I0011353

Automated Marketing with Webbots

By M. Eigh

ISBN-13: 978-1494913830
ISBN-10: 1494913836

Table of Content

Symbols Used in This Book

A book is a lousy form to use when I want to share a lot of secrets with someone else. I can't pull you close. I can't fist-bump or high-five you. You don't see it when I wink at you or roll my eyes. The nuances of my speech and messages of my body language are totally amiss.

But since I do not have a TV show, I will have to make do with a book. To make up for the intrinsic disadvantage of a book, I will be using the following symbols to help get my message across.

[Quote bubbles] sign indicates that I am introducing a technique or tool that falls into the *whispers* category.

[Crowd] sign indicates that I am introducing a technique or tool that falls into the *contagion* category.

[Spy] sign indicates that I am introducing a technique or tool that falls into the *espionage* category.

[Key] sign indicates that I am introducing a critical concept.

[Download] sign indicates a free download link for a tool of my suggestion.

[Magic] sign indicates that I am giving a tip.

[Paperclip] sign indicates a logical relationship between two segments of this book, but not a sequential one. If you are reading the ebook, you can tap or press the enter button to follow the sign. If you are reading the paperback, a destination page number will be provided.

[Binoculars] sign indicates it's time for you to roll up your sleeves and create a web use case scenario. Seeing is believing. You learn best when you watch it in action.

[Tools] sign tools I am not able to cover in details in this book but you should explore on your own and possibly add to your arsenal of web marketing.

[Notepad] sign indicates that we are dealing with an error-prone or easy-to-forget point and I would like you to make a note of it.

My Approaches

This book seeks to paint a realistic and accurate picture of the not-so-obvious marketing tools you can and should employ in your web marketing, Amazon's Kindle book marketing in particular. Amazon's Kindle book store is arguably the most intriguing and dynamic virtual marketplace in the world. I refer to it as the *Amazon Jungle* for obvious reasons. It is mysterious, dangerous and one has to acquire a particular set of skills in order to survive a journey therein, let alone to come out a crowd-cheered champion.

My analysis of the Amazon Jungle progresses along two dimensions. The first is akin to the focuses of physics whereby I break down the mechanical components of this marketplace. In doing so, I will invite you to roll up your sleeves and go under the hood together with me to get a feel. The second is akin to that of chemistry whereby I identify the forces that partake in this marketplace and the law of their interactions.

I hold these laws to be self-evident. But it is not possibly for you to fully observe these laws of fighting forces in the mere few hours you read through this book. That's why I will introduce many tools that enable you better cope with the dynamics of this marketplace. Without the salient perspectives presented in this book and the handy tools introduced, you could remain totally oblivious to forces that determine your fate in the Amazon Jungle. Think of me as your jungle tour guide, of the tools your night vision goggles.

A book like this has the clear and present danger of becoming another one of the laundry list type books swarming Amazon Kindle book store's Kindle authorship and web marketing categories.

I have no intention of inundating you with yet another tedious list of "you must do this" and "you must not do that" sage advices anyone can glean off the internet and repurpose into a book. When you give a man a fish, you give him one meal. When you teach a man how to fish, you give him a livelihood.

I am interested in the science and art of fishing; so should you. With this book, I intend to share with you all the secrets about the Amazon Jungle I have discovered and the counter-measures you can easily employ to boost your marketing. I have arrived at these discoveries because I have not been distracted by anyone's long list of advices. I allowed myself the chance to experiment and to learn from my own failures.

The Amazon Jungle is a humongus habitat. It's easy to see trees but hard to see the forest. A few decades from now, when we read Jeff Bezo's memoir, I'm sure we are all going to have some "oh, and that's why!" or "why didn't I think of that!"

moment when we look back. But for now, we are like the blind men examining an elephant in the ancient Indian tale, jumping to our own conclusions.

I am not so presumptuous as to assume that I am wiser than other Indies or self publishers who are roaming the Amazon Jungle just as zealously. But I do think I am methodical. From the very beginning, I have employed four unique approaches when I conduct my business on Amazon. These four approaches clearly have given me the power to perceive and observe things better. I will list these approaches as follows:

The **FIRST** of my approaches is inspired by a prescription from Taoism. Taoist masters such as Lao Tzu and Chuang Tzu asked anyone who was frustrated with life to learn from the example of water. Water adapts to any shape and never tries to defy gravity. More importantly, if you watch a creek meanders through a rocky hillside, you will notice that it always chooses the path of least resistance.

As an Indie author or self publisher, you are in the Amazon Jungle to make a fortune, a fame or, more realistically speaking, a living. Or at least a supplementary living. Your priority is to identify the easiest path to push forward, the path that presents the least obstacles.

This philosophy sounds convincing in theory but often gets ignored in practice. Your expedition through the Amazon Jungle consists of many short trips. Each of them has a clear objective: to get from Point A to Point B. None of them is trivial.

A typical example of a short trip is all the promotion you have to do when one of your books gets on KDP Select free promotion. Think of the 100 plus free book listing sites you have to submit your book to; think of the long list of free book promoters you have to Tweet to; think of the countless Facebook pages you have to wall-post to!

If you shirk these daunting tasks, you are not doing justice to your book. If you tough it out, it is humanly impossible: there is just not enough time in a day for you to complete all those form submission, Tweeting and wall-posting. Not to mention that most of us still have to hang on to our regular day jobs.

The sheer payload of the tasks presents an obstacle to your immediate journey. What do you do? You need to go around it. Not to cheat out of it by shirking the task of promotion, but by employing automation that handles the repetitive submission, Tweeting and Facebook posting.

Enter the bots. After all, this book is about web marketing with the help of bots.

The **SECOND** of my approaches is inspired by the existentialist proposition that existence proceeds essence. In plain English, if you could accord me the liberty of interpretation, this doctrine says whatever is there has a darn good reason to be there. It says none of the should-have's and could-have's matter at all. It says a brutal food chain has come into formation in the Amazon Jungle as the predators and preys, the herbivores and the carnivores, the strong and the weak, the healthy and the invalid, the beautiful and the ugly fight it out in a bloodbath. You have entered the Amazon Jungle *not* to seek justice from that food chain. You are there to make sure you don't sit at the bottom of it.

This approach may seem a bit cold-blooded and socially apathetic. But you are not alone if you take this approach. If you think Amazon has carefully designed and established this food chain, you are giving way too much credit to it. Amazon has merely provided the habitat, and benefitted from the life and death of the folia and fauna upon that habitat. If you become someone else' lunch one day, that someone else inches up a notch on the food chain and turns you into waste which fertilizes the habitat. Your thriving or demise benefits the habitat in any event. Amazon couldn't care less about your fate as an individual participant.

Every technological innovation pushes the human race into an unchartered moral and ethical frontier. Unless you close your eyes and see no evil, many of the battles you have to wage against your competitions in the Amazon Jungle present moral or ethical dilemmas for which you cannot find ready guidance in any textbooks. You may have the urge to consult your therapist or local priest about these dilemmas, but you will find it impossible to explain their premises.

One clear and present example is what's happening with the jewelers on Etsy. The moniker of Etsy is "Everything Handmade." But when jewelers employ 3D printing to make jewelry parts, are these jewelry still bona fide "handmade?" The Etsy puritans say "No!" The open-minded entrepreneurs who would like to gain competitiveness via 3D printing say "Yes!"

So which side is Chad Dickerson, CEO of Etsy, leaning toward on this issue? He has allowed the 3D printing practice to go on and defended it by saying: "These [3D printers] are the sewing machines of today. What they produce may not look handmade – or handmade in the Etsy definition – but the technology is marching so quickly."[i]

Obviously, if you happen to be a jeweler selling on Etsy and you happen to be a puritan, you are fighting an uphill battle.

Similar moral or ethical dilemmas are ubiquitous in the Amazon Jungle. If you dwell on your dilemmas, your competition will charge ahead of you, or eat you live for lunch. If your competitions are employing bots in their web marketing campaigns and you insist on not using the same, their productivity and efficiency is many times greater than that of yours.

At least for me, it helps to look at the Amazon Jungle from the existentialist perspective. It is the entire community's collective action that will define the future of Amazon. If you are feeling righteous morally or ethically, participate, don't just sit on the sideline, pointing fingers and pout. Bots have become an integral part of marketing now. If politicians can employ robocalls for their election campaigns, why can Indie authors employ some web bots to help sell their books?

And if there is an ethical way to employ bots in web marketing, you can help define that ethics with your action.

The **THIRD** of my approaches is inspired by the Pareto principle, also known as the 80-20 rule. The Pareto principle states that there is always an 80-20 relationship between effects and causes. This well-known dictum sounds more abstract than it really is. The best way to explain it is through examples and case studies.

Have you ever heard of the saying "If you want something done, ask a busy person to do it?" Well, the Pareto principle says the same – that in any organization, 80% of the work is always done by 20% of the workforce. Remarkably, history shows that many great thinkers have come up with brilliant observations that may appear to be simple applications of the Pareto principle.

For example, Dr. Sun Yat-sen, the founding father of Republic of China, once remarked that 80% of the Chinese people were snoring away under the feudal rule of the Manchu monarchy and that only 20% of them were awake. But the 20% would carry the Chinese Revolution to a success. History proved that he was right.

Vladmir Lenin, the founding father of Soviet Union and a purported "proletarian whisperer," deeply despised his proletarian mass followers. "The truth," Lenin declared, "is always in the minds of the minority."

As everyone who started using computers since the 80's know intimately, the Microsoft Windows operating system has been plagued with bugs ever since its birth. However, it has survived again and again. Legend goes that Microsoft preemptively employs the Pareto principle in fixing the bugs pertaining to each Windows release. The Microsoft teams pool the reported bugs and analyze their severity and correlation. They then select about 20% of those bugs to fix, knowing that on the strength of the Pareto principle, the rest of the 80% will either go away or not causing customers to cry murders anymore. Their strategy works every time.

I believe being conscious of the Pareto principle allows an Indie author to strategize web marketing better. It makes you look harder for those instruments that bring about the most reward. Apply the 80-20 rule to the entire collection of your published titles and you immediately realize that in the long run, 80% of your royalty income will come from 20% of the titles. The other 80% are just there as also-rans and for you to experiment marketing aggressive. Go ahead, for starters, pick one or two from the 80% pile and make them permanently free. If they are not bringing much royalty income, let them bring some attention and traffic to you!

The **FOURTH** of my approaches is inspired by Occam's razor which says that among competing hypotheses, the hypothesis with the fewest assumptions should be selected. Another way to interpret it is to say the easiest route from point A to point B is a straight line. Yet another way to interpret it is to say that simple methods always work better than complex one.

The world worships Sun Tzu as the ultimate war strategist and theorist. But few people know Sun

Tzu's Western rival, albeit not a contemporary one. This great rival is Carl von Clausewitz whose brilliant book *On War*[ii] remains a prime gem in the collective wisdom of human race.

One of the most prominent advices Clausewitz gives in that immortal book is "Always trust your first instinct." In the battlefield of any wars, commanders are always forced to make seminal decisions on basis of imperfect information. Clausewitz wants them to use Occam's razor to cut out all the *ad hoc* what-if's and endless second-guessing, and to stick with the first instinct which is their most natural reaction, not yet tampered by hypotheses.

Personally, when I think of Occam's razor, I basically follow the age-old folksy wisdom: If something sounds too good to be true, it is too good to be true.

Analyzing the web marketing battlefield where both human and bots are foot soldiers is not an easy task for me. My job is to cut to the chase and present you with an accurate breakdown of the normal marketing gimmicks: What are done by human and what by bots.

Those who utilize bots to replace human in a typical web marketing undertaking will never openly admit to you that they are using bots, lest you quickly play the catch-up game and wipe out their competitive advantage. But with Occam's razor, I can boldly identify the bots behind the human facades on many web marketing instruments.

I am able to arrive at many conclusions revealed in 🔗 Chapter Two: The Cocktail of Web Traffic because I am a staunch practitioner of Occam's razor.

What You Can Take Away from This Book

I lived in the Netherlands with my wife in the late 1990's, for about a year and a half. We spent half of our sojourn in Rotterdam and the other in Amsterdam. Looking back, that was one of the best times in our life. I truly cannot find one bad thing to say about that country and her beautiful people.

I was there in a pre-GPS age and to look for directions on the street, you did not tap the map on your phone, you accosted a stranger. When giving out directions, the Rotterdammers and Amsterdammers exhibited distinctive characteristics. Both were courteous and patient. But the Rotterdammers would overload you with auxiliary information you never asked for and distract you with other subjects. Simply put, the Rotterdammers took the opportunity to befriend you, offering excessive details that did not hurt but could be irrelevant or distracting. When you asked for the direction to a museum, you did not really ask for a tip on which mode of transportation to get there was cheaper. But a Rotterdammer would volunteer that.

The Amsterdammers, on the other hand, were concise when giving directions and never offer you more than what was *just enough*. Upon hearing their directions, you could immediately see in your mind's eye what turns to make and what landmarks to look for at each turn. When you said "Thank you" to an Amsterdammer who had just given you a direction, you truly felt that you could not miss it, as opposed to the warm and fuzzy feeling about a super-friendly Rotterdammer who had just left you cheerful but with too much information to digest.

In writing this book, I am that Amsterdammer who gives you enough information to reach your destination. I impart information on the twist and turns of your contemplated journey and what landmarks to look for in order to confirm your progress. If the path to your destination appears to be more challenging than you thought, I am merely being truthful and realistic. I apologize for not being that Rotterdammer who can chit-chat with you on many tangent subjects to put you in a better mood.

With equal certainty, I can assure you that I do not intend to micro-advise your web marketing. I will not give you advice on which side of a particular street you should be walking on in order to pass by the best espresso bar in town. Those are things you can explore at your leisure and liberty. After you read this book, I would like you to feel that you know enough to "get there," and that you "can't miss it."

If I have achieved that, I ask you to please post a book review on Amazon. Conversely, please do not hesitate to let me know at eigh.com@gmail.com if I have failed at my stated mission.

Chapter One Web Browser Imposters

1.1 Lingua Franca of the Internet

If you ask the average internet denizens what the lingua franca for the web is, I bet most of them are clueless. The typical response is likely a shrug. A shrug goes beyond "I don't know," it says: "Why should I care?"

You get a shrug from your yoga teacher who has just shown you her new WordPress blog. You get a shrug from your niece who, at the tender age of 11, has already acquired calluses on her thumbs from smart phones and tablets.

But if you want to be successful in marketing your products on the web, you ought to know what the lingua franca of the web is. You do not need to know the how's and why's and the how come's. But you need to know the characteristics of that lingua franca. You cannot begin to strategize your marketing without a keen awareness of those characteristics.

A picture beats a thousand words. I don't want to belabor an elaborative answer to the lingua franca question that is likely to bore you out of your skin. Instead, I would like you to listen – or watch, more precisely speaking – a conversation between your web browser and a website on the internet.

For the website, let's pick Amazon.com. For your web browser, let's pick Firefox. (If Firefox is not your most favorite browser, please just humor me this once. You can switch back to your beloved Chrome, Safari, Opera or Internet Explorer immediately after this exercise.)

First off, we need to take a page from NSA's playbook. We need to listen in on your Firebox's conversation with Amazon's web servers. Extraordinary objectives call for extraordinary tools. In this particular case, we need to download a web conversation interceptor called "Live HTTP Headers."

Using Firefox, please browse to `https://addons.mozilla.org/en-us/firefox/addon/live-http-headers/` and click on the "+ Add to Firefox" button:

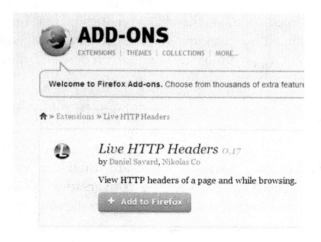

Depending on your network's and your browser's security settings, you may have to give Firefox explicit permission to install the add-on:

Once the add-on file is fully downloaded, you can press the "Install" button:

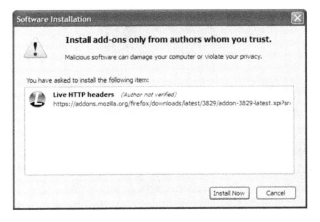

Answer "Yes" to Firefox's re-start prompt. Once Firefox reloads, browse to http://www.amazon.com. While you are still on Amazon.com, click on "Tool" on Firefox' menu bar and activate "Live HTTP Headers:"

Now you will see a popup window. Go ahead, click on something interesting on the Amazon.com homepage, or you can browse to a book of yours. Do your normal thing with Firefox main window and you will notice that your browser's conversation with Amazon's web servers being continuously captured in the "Live HTTP Headers" popup window:

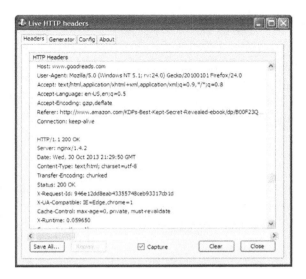

Two characteristics in these conversation logs are hard to miss. One is they come in blocks. The other is they generally start with the term "HTTP."

With just a little spying, we've successfully found the answer to the pressing question of the web's lingua franca: It's called HTTP.

HTTP stands for Hypertext Transfer Protocol. It is a protocol observed strictly by just about all computers in the world when they communicate with one another on the internet, with one playing the role of a server and the other that of a client. Namely, when two computers have a conversation on the internet, one normally serves as a website and the other the visitor.

By visually examining the conversation log, we also notice that these conversations are carried out in "chunks" or blocks. There are no "excuse me," or "can I get back to you on that?" There are absolutely no interruptions or interjections. The conversation is carried out in strict alternating sequence. Let's look at a typical conversation between a browser and a web server:

The web browser says: (For the sake of clarity, I have omitted the non-essential part of the dialog.)

```
GET / HTTP/1.1
Host: www.amazon.com
```

The web server says:

```
HTTP/1.1 200 OK
Date: Thu, 31 Oct 2013 00:44:09 GMT
```

Can you find a human communication parallel of this type of communication? If you haven't figured it out yet, allow me to enlighten you: It is as mechanical as walkie-talkie. The web browser says something and indicates, "Over." And the web server replies something and indicates, "Over."

This walkie-talkie like conversation pattern is a reflection of the most fundamental nature of the HTTP protocol. In the parlance of Information Technology, it is referred to as "stateless." In other words, neither the browser nor the web server bears any memory of what has just been covered in the dialog. Each "chunk" or block of message from the browser or server follows the exact same syntax and is constructed the same way mechanically.

To illustrate this point, we are going to do another exercise with Firefox Live HTTP Headers. But before we can get on with this exercise, we need to be able to tell what blocks of messages are issued by the browser and what by the web server. If you quickly browse through the log, you will notice many blocks that start with the verb GET or POST. Those statements are issued by the browser. In the HTTP protocol, commands like GET and POST are called verbs. Verbs are the speech pattern of web browsers.

Conversely, you will notice many statements or blocks of messages that start with following line:

```
HTTP/1.1 200 OK
```

The adjective OK is one of the descriptions a web server uses to communicate to a web browser. In the parlance of Information Technology, the combination of a 3-digit code and a description is referred to as HTTP Status Messages. If you are curious about the whole collection of status messages a web server can use, you can look at the details   here:
http://www.w3schools.com/tags/ref_httpmess
ages.asp.

But for the purpose of our exercise at hand, mission is accomplished as long as we can tell apart which statements were spoken by the browser and which were by the server.

Now scroll through your Live HTTP Headers log and locate a statement that start with the verb GET and bears an image in its URL (file path.) I have chosen the following for myself:

```
GET     /images/G/01/img13/digital-video-
games/bunkbed/8-16_dvg-batman-
ao_2_bunkbed._V354102086_.jpg HTTP/1.1
```

Typically, your browser would have loaded many images from the Amazon web servers so you should find it easy to locate a GET verb followed by a file path that represents an image.

Next, select that statement by clicking on it in the Live HTTP Headers window and hit the replay button:

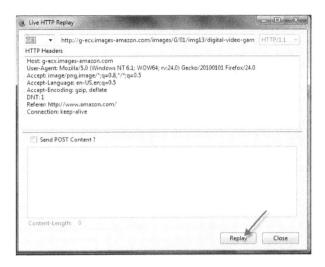

Live HTTP Headers immediately reconstruct the browser message for you. Once you hit the "Replay" button to confirm, you will notice that Live HTTP Headers has taken controls of your browser and has loaded the image into the window:

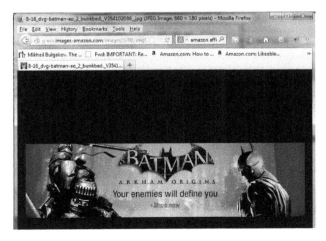

This is an image that should etch onto your memory and never fades. It tells you two shocking facts about HTTP:

1. Web servers have no clue if a dialog is initiated by a web browser or something else. It replies the same way. In the test we have just conducted, Live HTTP Headers initiated a dialog with Amazon's server, pretending to be the browser itself. Amazon's server played along.

2. It is easy to converse with a web server, as long as you obey the HTTP syntax. If you are an experienced coder, you can open a connection and start typing away your message. If you are not a coder and don't fancy the prospect of typing messages to a web server in compliance with HTTP syntax, there are tools out there to help you. Live HTTP Headers is just one very simple one.

The above exercise we have done is meant to be an eye opener. And the tool we have used is no more than a baby toy in the web traffic sniffer or web browser imposter arena.

For those of you who are inquisitive and ambitious, you can check out the following list of useful tools that can help you listen in on conversations between a web server and a web browser and also pretend to be a web browser at will. In other words, you can use them as your web spies and web browser imposters.

The following is a list of the well-known free web traffic sniffer and browser simulators on the market today.

Fiddler, http://fiddler2.com/ (Free)
TCPMon, http://ws.apache.org/tcpmon/ (Free)
WebScarab, https://www.owasp.org/index.php/Category:OWASP_WebScarab_Project (Free)
Vega, http://subgraph.com/products.html (Free)
Jmeter, http://jmeter.apache.org/ (Free)

1.2 The Magic Script

I will admit it upfront: There is no one single magic script. I'm dramatizing a phenomenon.

What exactly is the phenomenon am I dramatizing? After reading the last segment of this book, you probably have some inkling as to what it is. But allow me to spell it out for you as follows:

You have published a book and set up a Facebook fan page for that book. You want a lot of people to like that fan page. After a long day of hard work, you are pretty drained and are just farting around on the web. You remember that you had a few extra gmail addresses that you registered a while ago. You decided to use one and registered a new, fictional Facebook account, someone with the ideal persona of younger than you, of the opposite sex and really crazy about your book.

After the account is all confirmed and etc, you proceed to like your book's fan page on behalf of this new Facebook account. Just playing around to see what is possible. Just a test.

The like sticks.

Hmm. You start to think. What if I repeat this process five hundred times? Wouldn't I instantly have five hundred likes? Well, easy said than done: it's almost midnight and you've had a long day. So you table it for now and promise yourself to search the web low and high until you find all the resources and answers on this subject.

And if you do that, you are likely to find two most used automation tools on today's market.

1.2.1 iMacro

The first one is iMacro made by iOpus. iMacro is a tested top tool for web browsing automation, web data extraction and web testing. iMacro itself is a commercial platform and costs in the north of about $500 for a license. You can find out more about iMacro at iOpus' website: http://www.iopus.com/.

Whether you should purchase and use iMacro is entirely a business decision for you at a later stage. But for now, we need to get a taste of this software. iOpus does offer a free trial; however, if you are not an experienced software developer, the overhead of getting it to work so you can have a taste of it is hardly worth the trouble. Fortunately, there is a much easier way to try out iMacro.

iMacro offers a free add-on for Firefox. We all know how easy it is to use an add-on with Firefox. So let's install iMacro for Firefox and see what it can do.

Using Firefox, please browse to https://addons.mozilla.org/en-US/firefox/addon/imacros-for-firefox/ and click on the "+ Add to Firefox" button:

The rest is just a typical Firefox add-on installation process, which we went through in the previous section. You can 👓 review the procedures highlighted in 1.1 if you have forgotten. But it is pretty intuitive and you can just follow the prompts.

Once iMacro for Firefox is installed, you can activate or deactivate it by pressing the F8 key. Once iMacro is activated and you will see all the iMacro bookmarks in your Firefox' left panel. If it is a new installation for you, you probably only have a default bookmark called Current.iim. Underneath the bookmarks, you will also see three tabs that allow you to interact with any bookmark: Play, Record and Edit:

Please note that clicking on a tab that's labeled Play, Red or Edit *does not* start the action accordingly. The relevant action starts only when you press on the Play, Record or Edit button.

᠁ Now I would like you to browse to KDP's sign-in page at `https://kdp.amazon.com/self-publishing/signin`. Once the page loads in Firefox, please click on the Rec tab and press on the Record button. Next I would like you to log in as you do normally. Once you are in, please press the stop button and click on the Save button that's newly enabled and give your recorded web browsing episode a name to save it: (You have the carte blanche of nomenclature.)

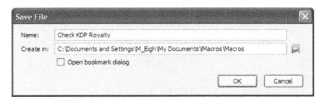

Next, I would like you to please log out of your KDP account and close down your Firefox. Make sure all Firefox tabs and windows are closed down.

Now start Firefox again and once your homepage loads – if your new tab defaults to a blank page, you do need to browse to a web page in order to activate iMacro – press F8 to activate iMacro. This time, you will see your previously recorded web browsing under the name you have given it. Go ahead, select that bookmark, and hit the Play button:

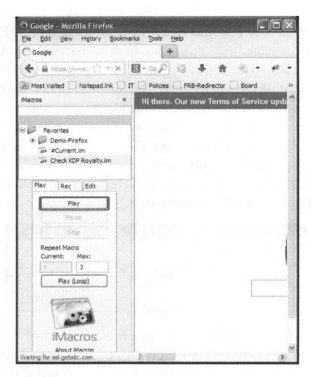

Now sit back and watch iMacro does all the log-in grunt work for you. Voila, you have just got your first magic script! Can you think of some similar grunt works you can delegate to iMacro? Of course you can. What about your emails? And your Facebook, Twitter, Instagram, GoodReads and a million other websites you have to sign in to frequent. Yes, before you explore other advanced ways to use iMacro, play around to get all your basic log-in's all automated.

Of course, what we have done here is truly a toddler's game in terms of what you can achieve with iMacro for Firefox or iMacro per se. Great minds think alike. If you can think of something to use it for, chances are someone else has already thought of it and created the script for it. Many coders and hobbyists create general purpose iMacro scripts. All you need to do is search low and high for it when an idea of automation tickles your fancy.

At the end of the day, if you have exhausted your search and could not find an existing free or for-sale iMacro you could leverage, hop on a fiverr.com type of sites and post your business requirement as a job. I am sure you will find many ready takers for the mission, at the price you set.

Here are three very active sites (marketplaces) where you can locate such talents to custom-generate automation for you:

```
https://www.seoclerks.com/
http://fiverr.com/
http://www.fivesquids.co.uk/
```

Of course, the clear and present use for any web browsing automation is for data scraping. If you have not given this any thoughts before, allow me to throw something on the table, just to get your mind going. This random idea is by no means suggestion of action you should take. It is presented here merely to illustrate the wide playfield you could gain by using web automation:

- Amazon Top Reviewers email addresses.

Amazon Top Reviewers all have profiles by default, even if there is no meaningful data displayed. Their profiles all starts with http://www.amazon.com/gp/pdp/profile/. And on their profile page, there is a universal label phrased as "Top Reviewer Ranking: [Number]." Some of them list their email addresses. Many of them do not. But with universal root of their profile URL's and the give-away label "Top Reviewer Ranking," you can easily construct an automation script to scrape the profiles.

Let's say you are interested in contacting those reviewers whose ranking is above 1,000 and whose profile page contains an email address, your script can easily set the aforementioned [Number] > 1,000 as a condition and crawls through all the profile pages. Every time the script detects an email address it records it for you in a file. At the end of the automation run, you will for sure harvest a few hundred Top Reviewer emails for you to blast out your book review request to.

Needless to say an automation web scraping script can be amateurish and crude or it can be sophisticated and seamless. A web scraper that only gets you a list of the Top Reviewers' emails without any metadata (such as the reviewers Amazon handle) is an example of crudeness. A scraper that not only gets you the email but also the reviewer's normal reading genre is an example of sophistication.

I could go on and on here with my own ideas. But I believe you have got the gist. Let your imagination takes to some new height. Where there is a will, there is an automation script.

1.2.2 uBot

The second candidate in the magic script category is uBot. I have chosen uBot as the second prominent example of web automation because of two reasons. One is its license model encourages resell of derivative products. As a result, you see hundred specialized uBot offspring targeting various social media platforms such as Facebook and Twitter. A lot of the mid to lower tier automation software for sale nowadays are no more than derivatives of uBot – the software themselves are created with uBot and are just a subset of uBot's features with targeted customization.

The second reason is that it appears (I have no supporting data to make any assertion either way) to handle CAPTCHA better. CAPTCHA stands for "Completely Automated Public Turing test to tell Computers and Humans Apart" and is the tripwire designed to trick automation script or bots on a website. Naturally, CAPTCHA presents a serious challenge to any automation that involves high volume web automation.

For example, in the aforementioned example of scraping Amazon Top Reviewers' email addresses, since there is no form submission and a visitor does not need to sign in in order to browse a reviewer's profile page, the automation can run without the danger of being stopped by a CAPTCHA.

However, if you are posting to the Facebook walls of 1,000 members of certain groups with an automated script, Facebook's server will stop you with a CAPTCHA once it detects an established pattern of repetitiveness.

If you browse online, you will find much more resources and discussion on how to beat CAPTCHA with uBot. Of course, the battle between good and evil is eternal. When uBot gains ground against CAPTCHA, servers dial up the difficulty level on CAPTCHA. It's the left foot vs. the right foot. Depending on your perspective, one of them is always playing the catch-up.

Unfortunately, there is not a browser add-on version of uBot we can play with. But take my words for it, it is another just as good, if not better, web automation tools you can use to boost your marketing and business intelligence.

Chapter Two: Web Traffic Cocktail

I characterize the web traffic to your Amazon book page, or any other product page of yours for that matter, as a cocktail because it is made with many ingredients. Some of them are obvious: people who have googled a subject and found your blog; they have clicked on links on your blog and been taken to your book page on Amazon. In the same vein, traffic can originate from your paid ads via Google AdWords, Facebook, YouTube and a hundred different other premium web outlets.

The less-known, albeit still obvious traffic comes from what I would describe as "involuntary clicks." For fear of being sued, I will not name names here. But there are many web advertising syndicates or outlets that use pop-ups, pop-downs, pop-overs, pop-unders, transitional ads, misleading buttons and rogue JavaScript-driven browser hijackers. I am assuming you have encountered these advertising tricks in your personal web browsing experience. But if you really don't know what I am talking about, all you need to do is browse through a few porn sites for 5 minutes. You will be bombarded with most of these kinds of ads, if not all of them.

Voluntary or involuntary, so far we are still talking about human traffic. They are *convertible* traffic. Convertible means they have the potential of turning into purchases of your product. It goes without saying that voluntary kind delivers a much higher conversion to you than the involuntary kind.

Traffic can be outright non-convertible. For example, if someone set up an internet café in Dhaka and offers visitors free internet access for 10 minutes if they first click on every links on a carefully designed "gauntlet" page. The café operator then turns around and sells those clicks at an unbeatable 1¢ per click on a PPC (pay-for-click) exchange. Needless to say that café operator does not ever reveal that there is absolutely no chance that any of the clicks could ever turn into purchases. Visitors who click on those ads could not afford internet connection, let alone any product sold on the internet.

If we turn the clock back by five to ten years, what I have just painted could be a realistic picture of the non-converting traffic landscape. Today, hardly any non-converting traffic is still generated this way.

Nearly 100% of non-converting traffic is machine-generated nowadays. In other words, non-converting traffic is almost completely bot traffic these days.

2.1 Jingling

There are countless pagodas in China. Jaded tourists like to say, "If you've seen one of them, you've seen all of them." Of all the general-purpose bot traffic generators, the Chinese-made Jingling is the most popular, prevalent and powerful. As of this writing, non-converting traffic generated with Jingling can still fool a vast majority of traffic tracking instruments or venues. Jingling is that one pagoda you must see.

As of this writing, based on my casual survey, there are at least a dozen sneaky vendors lurking around on eBay, SEOClerks.com, Fiverr.com and many other marketplaces selling Jingling under different rebranded names for about $20 a pop. If you come across with any of these vendors, do not waste your money. Jingling can be downloaded free and can be used easily, after you read this segment.

There are also hundreds, if not thousands of vendors on the aforementioned marketplaces selling delivery of traffic that come in quantities ranging from 1K to 100K or even unlimited. Don't waste your money on them either. Once you download Jingling, you can deliver the same quantity of traffic to yourself easily.

More importantly, Jingling is that one pagoda which allows us to instantly figures out all the other pagodas. Play with Jingling together with me in the following exercise and you can consider yourself graduated from the Non-converting Traffic Academy.

(As of this writing, Jingling only works on Windows. If you only work on Mac, please run Windows under Parallel so you can experience the wonder of generating non-converting traffic on your own!)

Please browse to http://www.spiritsoft.cn/. Since the page is in Chinese, you may be clueless as to how to find the software and install it. Please click on the button as shown in the screenshot:

In the next screen you will get the unpack password (as of this writing, it is just "123456".) It also informs you that Jingling is compressed into a WinRar file and if you do not have WinRar, you will need to download it free. It further asks you to white list Jingling if your anti-virus software blocks its installation. Assuming you are okay with all these, click on the "Flowspirit for Web Master" download button to get the rar file. "Flowspirit" is an interpretive translation for "Jingling:"

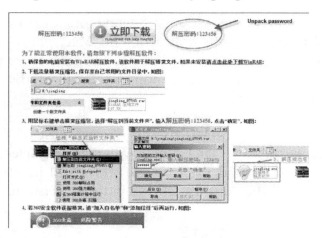

Once the rar file fully downloads you will be prompt to enter the unpacking password if you have chosen to open the downloaded file with WinRar. If you have chosen to save the downloaded file, you will have to click or double click on the WinRar file to get the password prompt. Once you pass the password check, you will see the only file in the rar folder is "Jingling.exe." Unzip it to anywhere you like and Jingling is ready to go.

Now locate where you have unpacked Jingling to and click to activate the program. Here's where the challenge lies: The entire program UI is constructed in Chinese. But no worry, I am going to walk you through as thoroughly as I can.

The main features of Jingling are represented in the three main tabs in its UI once the program loads:

Out of the three tabs, only the first two are relevant to users outside China. The third is only applicable to an instant messenger and micro-blog program by the name of QQ and made by Tengsheng.

For all general purpose traffic whereby you do not care about the *nominal* origins, how long a visitor stays on a page of yours and etc. The second tab is for tailored traffic whereby you can configure relevant parameters of the traffic pattern to suit a particular marketing purpose.

The first tab is easy compare to the second, all you need to enter are the URL's you designate to be the beneficiaries of the non-converting traffic you are going to generate with Jingling. The second tab involves some configuration. We will learn the details through the exercise below. Along the way, I will also introduce some new concepts that may answer some of your why's.

I am going to show you a typical application of Jingling: To artificially inflate the view counts of a web page. Jingling is good enough to fool pretty much any websites you can think of. For this demonstration, I have chosen eBay.

Page view counts are important for eBay sellers because eBay amplify its persuasive powers (whispers!) by displaying the view stats when a product page loads: (The following is a random example. Only high-traffic pages get promoted by eBay like this.)

The objective of our exercise is to increase the page counts of a product page on eBay. I am going to choose the same stranger's product page as the lucky beneficiary of our Jingling magic:

First, we record down the eBay product page's URL: http://www.ebay.com/itm/Sexy-Gypsy-Fortune-Teller-Pirate-esmeralda-disney-Fancy-Dress-Halloween-Costume-/370904864821?pt=US_Costumes&hash=item56 5ba71835.

Next, we shorten the URL using the free service provided by bit.ly. This shortening serves two purposes: 1) it is easier to enter it into Jingling. 2)

So we can track to see the traffic we are sending to this page via Jingling.

The URL gets shortened as http://bit.ly/1cyhUPu. If we suffix a "+" sign to the URL it becomes http://bit.ly/1cyhUPu+ which is the stats page corresponding to this particular shortened URL. Load that in our browsers we can see that there has been no clicks:

Next we activate the second ("Tailored Traffic") tab of Jingling and plug in our shortened URL:

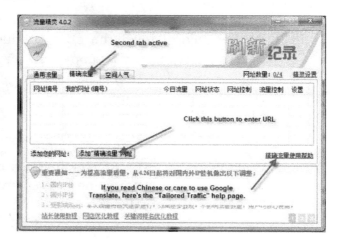

Now I will proceed to enter the bit.ly shortened URL. The following screenshot shows my entry details:

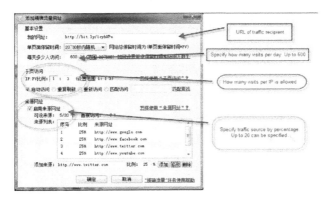

We will have to briefly review a few concepts before you can fully understand the entry details. But feel free to skip such drudgery if you are happy with just understanding the gist of it.

Page views vs. unique IP's. If you have used Google Analytics or other web metrics service before, you would know that just one of your friends spending a whole day clicking through your WordPress blog repetitively can boost the page views to whatever astronomical numbers humanly achievable. But the friend cannot do anything about the unique visit counts tallied as each unique IP (a computer's internet address) can count as just one visit. The setting in Jingling about "How many visits per IP is allowed" give you a chance to specify the page view to unique IP ratio. Since hundreds of millions of people use Jingling, the pool of their unique IP's is very large and even if you only allow one page view to be counted per unique IP, you will still get page views. The ratio you set here should be a reflection of your business requirement. In the case of our exercise, eBay counts each repetitive page load as a page view, regardless if it is from the same IP. So theoretically, we did not have to specify a page view to IP ratio, but Jingling has a maximum ratio of 1:3 allowed.

The reason Jingling has a 1:3 ratio cap is because of most prominent websites on the internet has floodgate control mechanism in place. If the same IP keeps issuing the same exact request, the server will automatically rejects. The reason for such practice is obvious. An online pollster must instigate floodgate control lest an extremely opinionated survey taker may choose to do the survey again and again till the result is rigged.

The next important configuration setting is the traffic source. You can tell from the screenshot that I have chosen Google, Facebook, Twitter and YouTube to share the credit of sending traffic to our chosen URL on equal basis. This is tied with the http_referer convention in server-browser conversation. It is akin to asking someone: "How did you hear about us?"

As a common practice, when a browser visits a web page, it lets the web server know the page that has referred it there, under the misspelled code name http_referer (the guy who drafted the protocol misspelled referrer as "referer" so the whole world is now stuck with http_referer.)

Due to the "stateless" nature of a HTTP conversation, servers do not validate the http_referer. It just takes the word of the browser for it. And in our case, since we are using Jingling to serve as our fake browsers, eBay server is just taking Jingling's word for it.

At this point, we have completed all due configuration and can just let Jingling go do its work. So we click on the "Confirm" button to start our newly configured traffic factory:

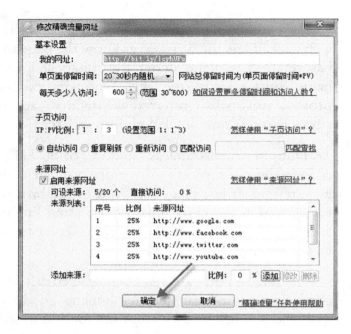

The other button next to "Confirm," of course, is the "Cancel" button. After letting it run a just a few minutes, we notice that traffic has already been accumulating:

But this is still kind of slow if I am just after traffic and couldn't care less what the fake source of the fake traffic is from. So I go into Jingling and deleted my entry in the "Tailored Traffic" tab and re-entered the URL in the "General Traffic" tab. The entry is easy as all you need is the URL:

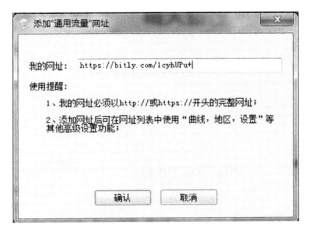

After this the traffic sped up and a merely ten minutes brought about big change in the stats:

And bit.ly's tracking engines sees nothing unusual and builds beautiful charts for our stats:

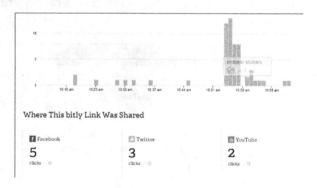

The geo-origins of the tallied traffic look normal as well:

Geographic Distribution of Clicks

Top Countries (clicks / % of total)		
United States		46%
Brazil		5%
Spain		3%
Indonesia		3%
Romania		3%
Philippines		2%
Ecuador		2%
Cyprus		2%
Belarus		2%
Canada		2%

There are many more details to the use of Jingling. These details fall outside the scope of this book. Up to this point, I believe we have successfully illustrated to ourselves the complexity and the secret ingredients of web traffic. If a lot of your web marketing needs call for the use of Jingling and you have to get into the fine tuning of this very versatile tool, feel free to email me with any questions at eigh.com@gmail.com.

To the average readers of this book, I do have to point out two features of Jingling that you should not miss:

1. In order to boost the traffic to one single target URL, you can use the four entry allowances to enter the same URL.
2. If it is required by your marketing mission, you can specify the geo sources of the traffic:

After a while, when we go back to check on that eBay page, the views per hour shows an expected increase:

If you have rolled up your sleeves intended to follow this exercise step by step, you should choose one of your eBay listing as the beneficiary.

2.1   Peeling the URL Onion

After learning the tricks of Jingling, we can't help feeling a bit invincible. If we could allow ourselves just one moment when we do not have to worry about ethics, terms of use that can come back and haunt you and other direct or indirect consequences, we sure will be overwhelmed with the infinite possibilities. Embarrassed about the low view counts on your YouTube video? Don't be. Just think about what Jingling did to an eBay listing and switch the beneficiary to your video.

Your short story just got published in an online ezine which is hosting a "Best Story of the Month" vote and your poor story is currently ranking an ugly 12th? No worry, just crank up an instance of Jingling and plug in your story's vote URL and let it run. (Well, don't let it run wild; or else your story will receive a total vote counts that come in higher than the ezine's normal traffic.)

But we do not live in that world void of ethics or consequences. Even if we do, there are some serious obstacles between Jingling and the things we would like to achieve.

First off, it's obvious we cannot add likes to our own Facebook pages with Jingling, or Twitter followers, or Amazon KDP Select free downloads. All such traffic must be generated from signed in accounts. Jingling does not appear to have a way to accommodate that. This is a subject we will delve deeper in 🔗 Chapter Three: Eureka! Then What?

Even for simple things like that ezine which is hosting an online voting for short stories, chances are they have used a WordPress plugin to handle the anonymous yet IP monitored voting. The voting submission mechanism is likely handled by an AJAX[iii] call in the page and wrapped deep in the innards of JavaScript.

As a matter of fact, finding the right URL for a bot to hit is the number one task and challenge for bot-based web marketing. Bots are not like human. They cannot analyze or react to a situation. They can only do what they programmed to do on a pre-determined URL.

To illustrate this point, we will go through an exercise together. At the end of the exercise, if you are still hazy on the methods and approaches used to obtain the crucial URL, it is totally fine. You only need to grasp the gist of it and the general impression that getting the URL you need is not always as straightforward as grabbing an eBay listing.

For this exercise, we are using my short story OSCAR'S TEN COMMANDMENTS published on   Everyday   Fiction   at http://www.everydayfiction.com/oscars-ten-commandments-by-m-eigh/.

Once you browse to the page and scroll down, you will see that my story did okay. It's got a 4-star rating based on 55 votes and there are a bunch of tweets, Facebook likes and g+ shares and 20 comments.

My objective now is to inspect the mechanism of voting interaction to see if I can find a simple URL for the 5-star vote. If I succeed, I could – at least in theory, and theory is what we are interested in in this book – plug in that URL in Jingling and let it run for a bit. And my story's rating should go up as a result.

For this exercise, we will choose Firefox as our designated browser again. We do so in order to leverage our previously installed Live HTTP Headers add-on.

 Now fire up Live HTTP Headers and hit the F5 key to refresh my story's page. You should be able to see the walkie-talkie style dialog between your Firefox and everydayfiction.com' server, like shown below:

At this point we will do two things to ensure that the stage is set properly for our next step. We need to press the "Clear" button to set blank canvas for new conversation. We also need to close other tabs, if any are open, to prevent any possible interference.

Next step I am taking is to hit the star to the very right so that I can give my story a five star rating. Now that strikes me as quite unethical, and I cannot really give myself such undue credit. So instead, we browse to SPEED DEMON AND CLOCKWORK DANCER by JR Hume at http://www.everydayfiction.com/speed-demon-and-clockwork-dancer-by-jr-hume/. This story is already way ahead of others and one more 5-star rating probably should not be too damaging to the stories behind it. I am doing this so that the process can be recorded and with the help of Live HTTP Headers, I may be able to locate the crucial URL to repeat that vote, with my own intended beneficiary. I clear the Live HTTP Headers panel again and submit the 5-star rating. I get the following log of HTTP conversations: (An easy way to get the entire relevant dialog but nothing more than that is to press the "Save all" button immediately after the action and give it a filename and location you can find.)

```
http://www.everydayfiction.com/stories/wp-
content/plugins/gd-star-
rating/gfx/loader/flower.gif

GET    /stories/wp-content/plugins/gd-star-
rating/gfx/loader/flower.gif HTTP/1.1
Host: www.everydayfiction.com
```

```
User-Agent: Mozilla/5.0 (Windows NT 6.1;
WOW64; rv:24.0) Gecko/20100101 Firefox/24.0
Accept: image/png,image/*;q=0.8,*/*;q=0.5
Accept-Language: en-US,en;q=0.5
Accept-Encoding: gzip, deflate
DNT: 1
Referer:
http://www.everydayfiction.com/stories/wp-
content/plugins/gd-star-
rating/css/gdsr.css.php?t=1368496262&s=a05
i05m20k20c00r05%23121620243046%23121620243
240%23s1pchristmas%23s1pcrystal%23s1pdarkn
ess%23s1poxygen%23s1goxygen_gif%23s1pplain
%23s1ppumpkin%23s1psoft%23s1pstarrating%23
s1pstarscape%23t1pclassical%23t1pstarratin
g%23t1gstarrating_gif%23lsgflower%23lsg&o=
off&ver=1.9.22
Cookie:
__cfduid=dfb02411dd642d696cf0403318170b566
1383411285714;        __qca=P0-2131791841-
1383411294691;
__utma=34586997.1486400467.1383411292.1383
411292.1383411292.1;
__utmb=34586997.10.10.1383411295;
__utmc=34586997;
__utmz=34586997.1383411295.1.1.utmcsr=goog
le|utmccn=(organic)|utmcmd=organic|utmctr=
(not%20provided)
Connection: keep-alive

HTTP/1.1 200 OK
Server: cloudflare-nginx
Date: Sat, 02 Nov 2013 17:41:12 GMT
Content-Type: image/gif
Content-Length: 1644
Connection: keep-alive
Last-Modified: Mon, 31 Dec 2012 18:48:27 GMT
Etag: "42cd328-66c-4d22a756836b0"
CF-Cache-Status: HIT
```

```
Vary: Accept-Encoding
Expires: Thu, 07 Nov 2013 17:41:12 GMT
Cache-Control: public, max-age=432000
Accept-Ranges: bytes
CF-RAY: c729d41c96a02b8
---------------------------------------------
----------------
http://www.everydayfiction.com/stories/wp-
content/plugins/gd-star-
rating/ajax.php?_ajax_nonce=ff62aca7f4&vot
e_id=11936&vote_value=5&vote_type=a&vote_t
pl=10&vote_size=46

GET    /stories/wp-content/plugins/gd-star-
rating/ajax.php?_ajax_nonce=ff62aca7f4&vot
e_id=11936&vote_value=5&vote_type=a&vote_t
pl=10&vote_size=46 HTTP/1.1
Host: www.everydayfiction.com
User-Agent: Mozilla/5.0 (Windows NT 6.1;
WOW64; rv:24.0) Gecko/20100101 Firefox/24.0
Accept: application/json, text/javascript,
*/*; q=0.01
Accept-Language: en-US,en;q=0.5
Accept-Encoding: gzip, deflate
DNT: 1
X-Requested-With: XMLHttpRequest
Referer:
http://www.everydayfiction.com/speed-
demon-and-clockwork-dancer-by-jr-hume/
Cookie:
__cfduid=dfb02411dd642d696cf0403318170b566
1383411285714;        __qca=P0-2131791841-
1383411294691;
__utma=34586997.1486400467.1383411292.1383
411292.1383411292.1;
__utmb=34586997.10.10.1383411295;
__utmc=34586997;
__utmz=34586997.1383411295.1.1.utmcsr=goog
```

```
le|utmccn=(organic)|utmcmd=organic|utmctr=
(not%20provided)
Connection: keep-alive

HTTP/1.1 200 OK
Server: cloudflare-nginx
Date: Sat, 02 Nov 2013 17:41:13 GMT
Content-Type: text/html
Transfer-Encoding: chunked
Connection: keep-alive
X-Powered-By: PHP/5.3.27
X-Robots-Tag: noindex, nofollow
X-CF-Powered-By: WP 1.3.10
Set-Cookie:
wp_gdsr_article=voted_%7C11936;
expires=Sun,    02-Nov-2014    17:41:13    GMT;
path=/
Vary: User-Agent,Accept-Encoding
CF-RAY: c729d41b96502b8
Content-Encoding: gzip
---------------------------------------------
----------------
```

Quickly glancing through the log, we can easily identify the crucial URL that made the voting happen is as follows: (It is also highlighted in the log with red fonts.)

```
http://www.everydayfiction.com/stories/
wp-content/plugins/gd-star-
rating/ajax.php?_ajax_nonce=ff62aca7f4&vot
e_id=11936&vote_value=5&vote_type=a&vote_t
pl=10&vote_size=46
```

This URL reveals everything. It tells us that the submission is done via AJAX ("_ajax_nonce=ff62aca7f4,") the story has a numerical id ("vote_id=11936,") the number of stars is determined by the key vote_value ("vote_value=5,") and, finally, there is a mysterious "vote_size=46" parameter whose meaning is not instantly clear to us.

A closer look indicates that there may be latency between submission and reporting. The story's rating summary says that the rating is based on a total of 42 votes. My guess is that there had been actually 45 votes prior to my vote a moment ago and that was why my vote was tagged as the #46. I cannot really call anybody there to confirm so I will give myself the benefit of doubt.

The next thing is I need to confirm my theory on the story ID ("vote_id=11936.") In order to confirm my theory, I view page source and global search the number "11936." I immediately find what I want to find, as follows:

```
<h1                          id="post-11936"><a
href="http://www.everydayfiction.com/speed-demon-and-
clockwork-dancer-by-jr-hume/"           rel="bookmark"
title="Permanent   Link:   SPEED   DEMON   AND
CLOCKWORK    DANCER    &#8226;    by    JR
Hume">SPEED   DEMON   AND   CLOCKWORK
DANCER &#8226; by JR Hume</a></h1></div>
```

This confirms that the vote_id parameter is just the WordPress Psot ID for the story. Which for my story, I can easily find the story ID is 11159. So to give my own story a 5-star vote, my educated guess is that the URL should be as follows:

http://www.everydayfiction.com/stories/wp-content/plugins/gd-star-rating/ajax.php?_ajax_nonce=ff62aca7f4&vote_id=11159&vote_value=5&vote_type=a&vote_tpl=10&vote_size=?

This URL string bears by story ID properly. The only uncertain part is the vote_size at the end which for now I put a question mark there. On my story page, the rating summary says the 4 stars rating is based on 55 votes. Based on our experience with the other story we voted on, it may be an inaccurate number. But to get the current accurate, server-determined vote_size is not hard at all based on our experience. All we need to do is manually vote once and trace the vote_size in Live HTTP Headers log and we get the next appropriate vote_size.

By now you probably have realized we have arrived in a dead alley. In order to use Jingling, we need to a pre-determined URL to enter into it. But in order to manipulate the WordPress voting plug-in, we have to increment a number at the very end of our URL.

As I emphasized, this demonstration is here for the purpose of illustration. I am not hell-bent on voting my story up the ladder. If I were, though, I could try many things.

I could try to disregard the value of vote_size= and just leave it like that and plug the URL in Jingling and see what happens. Worst case I fail to change the rating.

I could also try to write a "helper" script to increment the vote_size and automatically plug into Jingling for a one-time only execution. If you are a coder, you could think of many ways to get it done. Remember what I mentioned before? Where there is a will, there is an automation script.

But for the average readers of this book, the buck of the vote rigging exercise stops here. The conclusion is we cannot plug the URL into Jingling and beget ourselves some more 5-star ratings.

This example of limitation is here for a good reason. I want you to encounter an impasse in the book because you will encounter many in your real world web marketing. Equally important as a reason is I want you to move on to the next chapter, where I discuss getting web marketing with bots done through other people.

Chapter Three: Eureka! Then What?

We have ended the last chapter on a bit of a setback. But we have also had a journey with many revelations and epiphanies in this book up to this page. I totally understand it if you get the urge to yell "Eureka!" and to jump out of your bathtub, if you happen to be reading this book in your bathtub.

But I totally do not expect you to be the next Archimedes, to pound on your keyboard for a couple of days and to come up with a great web marketing bot. No, in my eyes, you are an entrepreneur. Once you understand the principle of web marketing with bots, you can get it done through other people.

To keep everything germane to the title of this book, this chapter focuses on the subject of how to create *contagion*, after we have fully discussed how to listen in on a browser-server conversation (*espionage*) and how to magically increase a product's page view count (the power of *whisper*.)

I have no desire of getting technical on the definition of contagion, but I think it is probably the most important aspect of web marketing that bots can play very a powerful role.

The power of contagion can be experienced everywhere. When you see a Facebook page with 500 likes, you don't really give it a second look. But you would pause and drill the page deeper if it has 80K likes. Same goes for a fellow author on Twitter who has 120K followers and a YouTube video that has 38K views and 1.5K thumb-ups.

Another example anyone who has done KDP Select free promotion knows intimately is the free download ranking. If a book ranks #19 in its category, its free promotion leaves almost no impact on its subsequent sales. Conversely, if a book runs up to #4 in free download in the entire Kindle store, you bet swarms of people would still chase down the book after its free period has ended to take a look. Many of them will decide to pay the piper and actually buy the book. We humans are all susceptible to herds' mentality. We are slaves to peer pressure.

And later in this chapter, we will get to look at cheap and easy ways to create contagion with bots.

3.1 ⁕ Standardized Happiness Package

Are you the type of person who reads the installation manual carefully before you put your new home entertainment equipment or furniture together? Or you just roll up your sleeves and go right at it, consulting the manual only when you have to or are in trouble? Do you prefer granular instructions or you prefer IKEA style word-less diagram?

Either way, I think you agree with me when I say that the fun starts when you are putting the parts together.

We have so far learned how easy it is to spy on our browsers' data transaction with a web server, and to manipulate it to our advantage. We have learned the secret ingredient in today's web traffic cocktail – the non-converting traffic which is mainly generated by bots. We have also looked closely at a couple of the most well-known web browsing automation tools. I would say that it is quite reasonable if you feel you can make do anything with the newly acquired knowledge.

However, in the IT world, putting the parts together is much harder than building the individual parts. Need any proof? Just look at the Obamacare portal site healthcare.gov. After half a billion dollars spent on separate components that were farmed out to individual contractors, it bombed miserably the moment the parts were put together.

Yes, you have acquired all the crucial knowledge you need to devise and construct your wonderful web marketing bots. But there is still a steep learning curve. It is pretty safe to assume that your tuition won't be as steep as half a billion dollars but you would definitely lose a lot of time – time you could spend authoring or publishing books and marketing them.

So my advice to you is to outsource. For illustration purposes, I will use social media as an example area whereby you can outsource and get your intended contagion created.

Cheap IT hubs are all outside US. Most of social media contagion expertise vendors are from these hubs: India, Pakistan, Turkey, Bulgaria, China and … you name it. These vendors lurk around the Fiverr.com type of sites. So when you have a web marketing campaign to run and need to boost your social media profile to ooze some power of contagion, you will need to check these sites out.

There are many marketplaces that fit the bill, but check out the following three first so you get a yardstick on the pricing level and a general sense of what are available for sale.

https://www.seoclerks.com/

```
http://fiverr.com/
http://www.fivesquids.co.uk/
```

I am far from an expert on these kinds of marketplaces but my feeling is that for a couple of dollars, you can easily get Facebook likes, Twitter followers or YouTube video views in the hundreds. If you have a budget of $10 or $20 we are talking about likes, followers and views in the tens of thousands. If you are willing to plop down $100 you can have 100K followers the next morning for sure. However, this is really the area where all the questions can only be worked out between you, your ambitions and your ethics. And maybe also your God, if you are a religious person.

Automation can also be farmed out. Three hundred free Kindle book promotional sites to submit to and you do not have time to handle it while not able to work out a script? No problem, somebody on those sites may just be able to deliver satisfactorily or come close, after you post your requirement as a job to hire.

Use what you have learned in this book as your bargaining chips. You know the folks you are dealing with are basically using software to generate the work. You know at the end of the day whatever they deliver to you are all bots or bot-generated, despite all their claims to the contrary. So don't overpay for anything. Don't ever feel guilty for only paying $1 for 200 Facebook likes, because the guy only spend half a minute running a script to send 200 likes from 200 Facebook bots.

There is one thing I would advise against purchasing and that is non-converting traffic. You know how easy it is to generate it with Jingling. So if your objective is to boost your blog's traffic ranking with Alexa, crank up your Jingling and do it yourself. Save that few bucks you spend buying those non-converting traffic for the gift copies of books you need to send to the Amazon Top Reviewers.

Fulfill your social media contagion needs by outsourcing is a complicated matter with sometimes unpredictable results. That's why I have chosen an oxymoronic title for this segment of the book: Standardized Happiness Package.

It's ironic because happiness cannot be standardized. But in the age of web marketing with bots, happiness are being packaged and hawked.

This title is inspired by a title used by Charles Yu for his rather famous Sci-Fi short story, "Standardized Loneliness Package."[iv]

3.2 👫 Snake Head or Dragon Tail?

The Chinese have a saying: Be the snake head, not the dragon tail. A snake is no comparison to a dragon in terms of grandeur. But at least you are the head.

Another way to interpret this folksy saying is always be among the first few to jump on a bandwagon when a new phenomenon is trending. In the age of web marketing with bots, a lot of the rules and trends reflect the nature of IT industry.

The IT industry has two unique characteristics: It changes fast and it often chokes on refactoring. Refactoring is IT's fancy way of describing a retroactive change. Its fast change means whatever bot-based marketing technology is always going to be short-lived. Its choke on refactoring means you may just be lucky enough to be grandfather-provisioned for a while if you were the first users of that technology, since riding it may require an overall system outgrade.

Such backdrop gives you an idea: When your inspiration leads you to innovative bot-based web marketing schemes, do not hesitate. Make a decision on whether to use it or now. If you decide to use it, follow the Nike motto: Just do it!

Whatever you can do this week may not be permitted next week. Not too long ago, authors can enter HTML straight up in the KDP book description editor. That boat soon sailed and authors have to use a special workaround to get HTML into their book description. (See details in my book *KDP's Best-Kept Secret Revealed: How to Embed Videos and Widgets in Your Book Description*.) Now it looks like Amazon will soon make this workaround obsolete too. But if you have jumped on the each of the HTML ship early, you have enjoyed a good ride.

What is the latest ship on web marketing with bots as far as Amazon book marketing is concerned? It is ... Are you ready?

It is bot-downloads. Yes, you heard me right. It's bot-downloads that you can schedule to happen on your KDP Select free promo days. The bots hit your book's download link with a vengeance. You see 2K download in your KDP report, then 5K, then 10K and then 30K.

Before you know it, your book will rank in the top three of free downloads in Amazon Kindle store. Then you push the delete button right around 6:00 PM Eastern before your free day expires at midnight Pacific. That gives your book a good four to five hours to hang around in the first page of Kindle free books, albeit with a non-zero price and Amazon's standardized mea culpa note "Why is this not free?"

And many of those who came to your book with the initial plan of getting it free will end up buying it. And there are thousands per hour who come to that page.

"How do I do bot-downloads?" I can almost hear you ask. The answer I give is two-folds. First of all, it is possible because Amazon is divided into the following eleven territories:

Amazon.com
Amazon.co.uk
Amazon.in
Amazon.de
Amazon.fr
Amazon.es
Amazon.it
Amazon.co.jp
Amazon.com.br
Amazon.ca
Amazon.com.mx

Out of the eleven, Amazon.com is the default catch-all. So if a country does not have a designated Amazon domain, the shoppers there will be routed to Amazon.com. And there are a lot of countries in the world.

It is quite natural for us to equate Amazon.com to be the designated home territory for U.S.A. While that may be true in terms of where most of the buying customers are coming from, it is not necessarily the case when it comes to a book's free download. When an Amazon account holder in Saudi Arabia, Qatar, Pakistan, Turkey or Korea downloads a book of yours, it goes under Amazon.com.

And that's where most of the magic lies. Thousands of Amazon.com bot accounts are being established by automation process. These accounts never purchase anything. They are bot hoarders of free ebook. At some automation script's command, they swarm a book's page and download it. The author gets the promotional benefit. The author pays the bot operator. It's that simple.

Secondly, this is technologically possible. If you have any doubt, you only need to look back at the WordPress star rating submission analysis we did in ∞ Chapter Two. It's basically the same challenge, with some added complexity resulting from account signing-in. Nowadays, if a download is specified to go into an account's CloudReader, no physical book data needs to be transferred. That just makes bot-downloading super simple.

So, should you invest the time and money to invent your own free book downloading bots? Well, think of the Standardized Happiness Package.

"So who are offering these promotional services?" I can hear you ask.

Look around. Search hard and you will find them.

"Why can't you tell me who they are and where to find them?" You ask.

Well, I cannot tell you who they are and where to find them because I would be accusing those people of doing bot-downloading if I do. I have no intention of getting into a fight with anyone, let alone a legal one.

Remember, I don't have proof; I don't care about the proof; I trust my first instinct and, I have Occam's razor.

Reprise

This book is not a conspiracy theory. I am not trying to shock you with an "A man just bit a dog" story. If you are shocked at the reality of web marketing with bots, it's because you come from a "see no evil" world. But we live in the same world and I am glad I get to present my perspective to you in this book.

I did a similar thing decades ago in Amsterdam, to our downstairs neighbor Lykla. Lykla had biked around Amsterdam all his life and knew the streets of Amsterdam like the back of his hand. One day, my wife and I had a party to go to and we learned that Lykla was going to. So I offered him a ride in my company-assigned Rover. Lykla immediately came up with the most efficient zigzag routing through the belly of Amsterdam to get to the destination. I believe nobody could have come up with anything better if we were to cut through Amsterdam.

But I offered an alternative routing: What if we just took the Ringweg (the A10 expressway, a ring around Amsterdam.) That way we could get to the south of Amsterdam from the North in ten or twenty minutes and our destination would be just blocks off the Southwestern section of the Ringweg.

Lykla was shocked. He was conceptually aware of the Ringweg. However, since he never drove, he had not realized one could actually take advantage of it to get from one part of Amsterdam to another.

When I think of you, my reader, I could not help thinking of Lykla. I am sure you are more or less aware that there are bots on the web. But I bet you have never realized you could put them to use for yourself too.

Whether or not you engage in any web marketing with bots is a decision entirely up to you. After all, at the end of the day, you are accountable for your decisions in your web marketing. I am thrilled if the perspectives and information in this book has made an impression on you.

If you like what you have read in it, please post a book review on Amazon for me. And if you have any follow-up questions for me, feel free to reach out to me at eigh.com@gmail.com.

[i] *Etsy CEO talks offline retail, people power and 3D printers as the new sewing machines*, Stuart Dredge, theguardian.com, June 5, 2013

[ii] On War, Princeton University Press; 1st edition (1984)

http://amzn.to/1aMQ0hw

[iii] AJAX stands for asynchronous JavaScript and XML. Check its Wiki entry for more details.

[iv] *Standard Loneliness Package*, by CHARLES YU, NOVEMBER 2010 Lightspeed